The Red Deer

Brian Staines

BLANDFORD PRESS
Poole   Dorset

Contents

Illustration Credits

Cover Geoffrey Kinns; M. Clark page 35; Dr. T. H. Clutton Brock 18; R. P. Cummings 2; H. Kinloch/Aquilla frontispiece; G. Kinns 19; L. MacNally 30; B. Mitchell 3, 10, 11, 15, 23, 26, 38; T. Parish 39; B. Staines 2, 6, 7, 10, 11, 18, 34, 42.

Picture Editors Michael Clark David Corke

Art Work Michael Clark

First published in Great Britain in 1980 by Blandford Press in association with The Mammal Society.

Copyright © 1980 Blandford Press Ltd
Link House, West Street
Poole, Dorset BH15 1LL

ISBN 0 7137 0898 0

British Library Cataloguing in Publication Data

Staines, Brian W
  The red deer.
  1. Red deer – Juvenile literature
  2. Mammals – Great Britain – Juvenile literature
  I. Title   II. Mammal Society
  599'.7357   QL737.U55

Printed in Great Britain by Purnell & Sons Ltd, Paulton (Bristol) and London.

Introduction

Red deer are the largest wild animals in Britain. They can be seen throughout England either in parks or living free, but are commonest on the mountains and moorlands of the Scottish Highlands, where large herds can be seen grazing the sweet summer grasses or collecting around what little shelter is available when winter storms drive them onto the lower ground. Secretive and wary, their rusty brown coats blending perfectly with their surroundings, they are not easily seen by the casual visitor. Their keen senses allow them to detect us long before we are aware of their presence. But, with care and patience, and a good pair of field glasses, they can be seen, particularly in the early evening when they come down from the hillsides to feed on the rich grasses in the valleys.

From prehistoric times to the present day there has been a close relationship between man and red deer. They played a vital part in the life of early man, their flesh providing him with food, their skin with clothing and their bones and antlers with tools and weapons. Later, as great beasts of the chase, they were hunted by king and noblemen, and then, when agriculture and forestry grew in importance, they became as a nuisance, damaging our crops and eating our newly-planted trees. They have now been domesticated to become our newest 'farm' animal.

We have to reconcile the fact that red deer are a valuable resource and part of our national heritage with the fact that they are also unwanted as an uncontrollable pest. The more we understand how this magnificent animal lives and behaves the more likely we are to be able to do this.

Names

The scientific (Latin) name for the red deer, or noble

Red deer country in the central Highlands. Red deer were once woodland dwellers throughout Britain but today are most numerous on the exposed, often treeless mountains and moors of Scotland.

Red deer are now colonising many forestry plantations in Scotland. The closely planted trees give them good protection from weather and disturbance, and the many open areas provide ample food.

Stags boxing. The new growing antlers are soft and easily damaged, so stags fight by kicking at a tremendous rate with their fore-legs.

deer, is *Cervus elaphus*. It belongs to the mammalian order Artiodactyla (the even-toed hoofed mammals) and to the family Cervidae. Cattle and sheep belong to the family Bovidae.

Red deer evolved in central Asia some 5-10 million years ago and have spread around the world. Those that spread westwards gave rise to the 'typical' red deer we know in Britain and those going eastwards became the Asiatic and North American wapiti *(Cervus canadensis* or *Cervus elaphus canadensis)*. There are about 16 subspecies surviving today, although some, like the Shou of eastern Tibet and Hangul of Kashmir, are becoming very rare. Red deer will interbreed with wapiti and also the introduced Sika deer *(Cervus nippon)*. Sika/red hybrids are found in parts of north-west England and the two have interbred so freely in Wicklow (Ireland) that it is doubtful if any true red deer exist there. We do not know if hybrids occur in Scotland but, if so, this could threaten the survival of the native species.

The male red deer is called a stag and the female a hind; the young up to one year old are called calves. We call a male wapiti a bull and the female a cow. Wapiti are also known as 'elk' in North America, and may be confused with the European elk *(Alces alces)*, so we now call *Alces* moose on both continents.

A hind that is suckling a calf is called a milk hind, and an adult without a calf is called a yeld, or sometimes eild or blue hind.

Because of man's interest in hunting deer, a special vocabulary has grown up which may vary from place to place. Animals of different ages, for example, have various names:

Age	Male	Female
1st year	stag calf, veel calf	hind calf
2nd ..	brocket, broacher, knobber or spiker (depending on the form and size of the antlers)	brocket's sister, hearse
3rd ..	espayard, spayard, brock	biche, bise
4th ..	staggard	hind
5th ..	great stag or great soar	hind
6th year and older	hart	hind

A stag becomes 'warrantable' (suitable for hunting) in its sixth year.

Field Signs

Because deer are secretive, we often have to look for signs to know whether they are in an area.

The droppings, or 'fewmets', are black or brown,

about 20 mm long and 10 mm in diameter; in summer they sometimes stick together. Their tracks, or 'slots', are typical of cloven-hoofed mammals and are about 7 cm wide at the heel.

The presence of red deer can also be detected from wallows. These are usually peaty or boggy places where both stags and hinds roll and trample; they are used from April to October but particularly when their winter coats are being shed and during the breeding season, or rut, when they are much used by stags.

Thrashed trees are another sign that deer are about. Stags rub or 'thrash' trees or shrubs to clean their antlers of velvet in summer and to advertise their presence during the rut. The bark of thrashed trees is shredded, usually 60-120 cm above the ground, and the side branches are generally broken. Bark is also eaten, but the stems of barked trees do not have the same tattered appearance as thrashed trees. All the large deer in the British Isles eat bark and the males thrash or fray trees, so it is difficult to identify the particular species from these signs alone when more than one is present.

Description

The adult is a large red-brown deer without spots. It has a large creamy-white patch on its rump which extends upwards a little surrounding a relatively short tail (about 20 cm with hair). This patch is less well-marked than in sika and fallow deer and not usually so clearly bordered with black.

Red deer have two seasonal coats. The summer coat is usually reddish-brown, sometimes dark brown or yellowish and rarely white or piebald. Moult into the winter coat starts in September and is usually over by December. This coat is darker, usually brown, but may be blackish, grey, reddish-brown, fawn or again white

Red deer eat the bark of many different types of tree, in this case lodgepole pine (Pinus contorta). This damage is very costly to foresters.

Deer topiary. By persistent browsing on favoured trees like this Norway spruce (Picea abies), deer not only hold back growth for many years but often create bizarre shapes.

or piebald in a few individuals. It has a thick layer of underwool 20-25 mm long. Moult into the summer coat starts in April to May and is usually over by August. So a red deer is, in fact, 'red' for only a very short time in the summer. A dark line is sometimes found down the neck and back, occasionally with spots on either side. The belly is off-white to grey.

Most calves are born from mid-May to the end of July, and are usually brown, reddish or fawn, with white spots on the neck, back and flanks. They have two moults, the first usually within two months of birth produces a fluffier version of the adult summer coat. The winter coat is seen from October to November onwards.

There are many folk tales about the white stag. In some parts of Scotland they are thought to contain the soul, or to be the reincarnation of a previous laird or lord. In other areas they are thought to be an ill-omen and that a death will occur. But when you see a 'White Hart' public house or inn, this White Hart was part of the coat of arms of Richard the Lionheart of England, and nothing to do with local natural history or ghosts!

Like other animals that chew the cud (ruminants), red deer do not have any upper incisors but a horny upper pad upon which the lower incisors close to crop the vegetation. The milk teeth on each side consist of a pointed canine and three cheek teeth (pre-molars) in the upper jaw; in the lower jaw there are three incisors, an incisiform canine and three cheek teeth. These are all replaced by the end of the second year with the permanent teeth which can be told from the milk ones as they have only one cusp each, whereas the third lower milk pre-molars have two cusps each.

The plants deer eat are hard and coarse and wear down the teeth quite quickly, so by comparing the amount of wear, particularly on the cheek teeth, we get

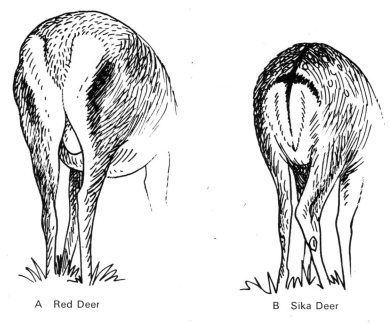

A Red Deer

B Sika Deer

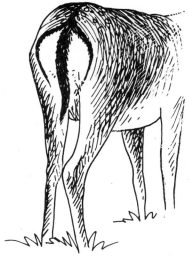

C Fallow Deer

Fig. 1 *Characteristic rump patterns of red, sika and fallow deer. The rump patch in red deer is less well marked than the other two species, and the tail is shorter.*

9

Stags cast their antlers each spring. The new ones start to grow within a couple of weeks.

In late June the antlers are well grown and the summer coat is starting to show through. These stags will soon leave the valley bottom for the higher ground.

When the velvet dies and the antlers harden, the loose, dead skin clearly irritates the stag and he thrashes his antlers against trees and other vegetation to get rid of it.

Stags also thrash trees and shrubs during the rut, sometimes so vigorously that the tree is killed.

a good idea how old an animal is. Another, more complicated way is by cutting one of the cheek teeth in half (the first in the lower jaw is best) and polishing it. Beneath the roots there is a little pad of dental cement and, if you use a magnifying glass, you will see white and opaque rings. Just like the rings on a tree, these are laid down every year so by counting them we can see how old an animal was.

Antlers

Antlers are unique to the deer family. Cattle, sheep and antelopes have horns which they keep and which grow throughout their life; a deer's antlers are shed or 'cast' and new ones grown every year.

Only the stag has antlers, and they grow from bony outgrowths called pedicels on the frontal bones of the skull. Pedicels do not usually develop in calves before 10 months in Scotland. The first antlers in Scottish deer are usually no more than knobs beneath the skin or short spikes; in deer-parks these first antlers may fork at the top. Animals reared indoors on good food grow antlers as calves.

The antlers are cast from mid-March to July, older stags and those in good condition casting first. The new antlers start to grow within a couple of weeks. These 'antlers in velvet' are soft and well supplied with blood. By late July to September this blood supply is cut off, the antlers harden, and the skin or 'velvet' dies. This obviously irritates the stag and he thrashes his antlers vigorously against trees or shrubs to rid himself of the loose, dead skin. The antlers are 'clean' of velvet by mid to late August in adult stags, but often not before October in the youngsters.

The antlers become larger and more complicated as the animal gets older, being biggest when stags are 9-11

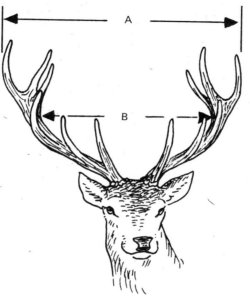

Fig. 2 *Antler measurements usually made in Britain.*
Key: A *'spread'—the widest outside measurement.*
B *'span'—the widest inside measurement.*
C *'length'—measured from the tip to the coronet along the outside of the antler.*
D *'beam'—the smallest circumference between the bay and tray tines.*

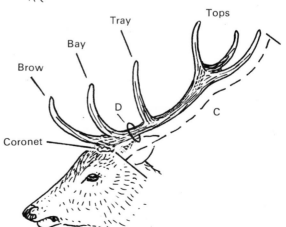

years old. The first points (nearest the head) are called 'brows', followed by 'bays', then 'trays' and finally 'tops'. The average number of points or 'tines' of Scottish deer is around 8, but antlers with more than 20 have been found. Red deer from continental Europe or those living in deer-parks usually have a greater number of points, the most recorded from Britain being 47, from a stag at Warnham Court deer-park, Sussex. One from Germany had as many as 66.

Stags with various numbers of antler points are given different names. A 'royal' stag is one with 6 points on each antler—brow, bay, tray (called 'his rights' in south-west England) and three points on the top; if a stag has any other combinations of 12 points it is referred to as a 'twelve-pointer'. A stag with 13 points is sometimes called an 'Imperial' and one with 14 a 'Monarch'. One that has no lateral points is known as a 'switch'. Some stags do not develop antlers at all; these are called 'hummels' or, in south-west England, 'notts'. They are not uncommon in Scotland. There is no single explanation for hummels, and there are several types. Some may be infertile stags that had some injury to the sex organs when they were calves and never developed pedicels. Others have pedicels, but antlers never develop or they may only grow very small 'buttons' each year. Some hummels are able to breed and hold a harem of hinds during a rut. However, contrary to opinion held often in the past, hummels are not much bigger than antlered stags of a similar age.

Antler growth is linked with the yearly cycle of sexual activity. A high concentration of the hormone testosterone (which is produced by the testes from August to April) stops antler growth, allows the shedding of velvet and keeps the antlers in 'hard horn'; low levels (April to August) allow the antler to be cast and grow again in velvet. So a stag calf that is castrated, or 'cut' as the

14

Red deer are incredibly agile and fleet of foot over the rough, hill land. They are forever alert, and their keen senses allow them to detect danger from a long way off.

Victorians put it, never grows antlers. If older animals are castrated when the antlers are growing, the antlers remain, but always in velvet; if castrated when in 'hard horn', the stag will first cast his antlers then regrow them, but again these will always stay in velvet. These antlers do not have many tines, if any at all. So, clearly, other hormones are involved, that affect shape for example, but these have not yet been found.

Many cast antlers are eaten by red deer in Scotland, but not, apparently, so much elsewhere. This probably reflects the poor quality food available, and it may supply minerals, particularly phosphorus, which is in short supply. Some antlers are chewed when still on the owner's head!

Measurements
Red deer vary in size and weight according to the sort of

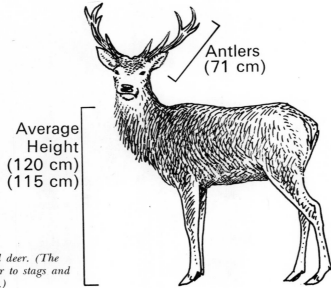

Antlers
(71 cm)

Average
Height
(120 cm)
(115 cm)

Fig. 3 *Size of red deer. (The higher figures refer to stags and the lower to hinds.)*

places where they live. An average hill stag weighs about 110 kg (live weight) and yeld hinds 75 kg, 10 kg heavier than milk hinds. Deer from woodlands are often much heavier, stags from Grizedale Forest in the Lake District, for example, weigh around 195 kg and hinds 95 kg. But even these weights do not compare well with red deer from continental Europe, those in Yugoslavia and Hungary being 2-2½ times as heavy as Scottish hill deer.

Typical stags from hill country in Scotland will stand up to about 120 cm at the withers and are 200 cm from the tip of the nose to the tip of the tail. Hinds are up to 115 cm tall and 180 cm long.

Stags are in best condition in late September but lose about 17% of their body weight during the breeding season, or rut; they can lose another 20% or more during winter. Hinds are fattest in November and in poorest condition in late winter.

Red deer in Scotland today are much smaller than

Average Live Weight
  (110 kg)
  (75 kg)

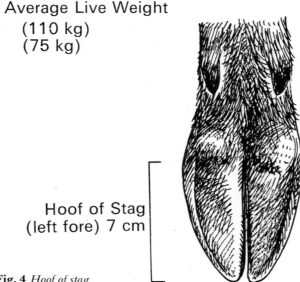

Hoof of Stag
(left fore) 7 cm

Fig. 4 *Hoof of stag.*

17

A group of hinds and followers.

Although usually wary, red deer do become accustomed to people. One stag from this group used the caravan as a back-scratcher—even though it was occupied at the time!

18

Hinds fighting.

their Iron Age ancestors. In recent times this has been due to the poorer habitats they have been forced to live in since the forest clearances, for calves of wild deer that

Fig. 5 *European range of red deer. Because of hybridisation with sika deer, no true red deer may still exist in Wicklow (Ireland).*

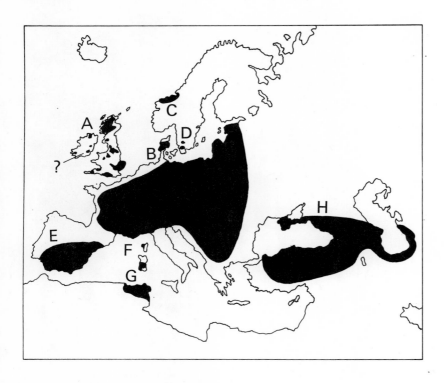

Key:

A— *Cervus elaphus scoticus*
B— *C. e. hippelaphus*
C— *C. e. atlanticus*
D— *C. e. elaphus*
E— *C. e. hispanicus*
F— *C. e. corsicanus*
G— *C. e. barbarus* (Barbary deer)
H— *C. e. maral* (Maral)

20

have been caught and reared in captivity grow much larger than their wild parents.

Distribution and Habitats

Red deer are still widespread in Europe and are found from just south of the Arctic Circle in Norway to North Africa. They live from high alpine meadows to lowland pastures, and all types of woodlands. They have been introduced into Argentina, Chile, Kentucky, Australia, and particularly in New Zealand where they are now widespread and numerous.

Although once common throughout the British Isles, the greatest concentrations now occur in the Scottish Highlands and Islands, about 255,000 living on $2\frac{1}{2}$ million hectares of hill land. Numbers are low elsewhere except for Exmoor (about 600-800), north-west England, East Anglia, and south-west Ireland.

Apart from those in the British Isles, red deer are animals of the woodland edge. However, in the Scottish Highlands, and perhaps also in Exmoor, and Martindale in north-west England, they are found on areas with few or no trees at all. Red deer were originally woodland dwellers in Britain also, but since early times our native woodlands have been cleared for timber and for agriculture, and deer have been pushed onto the exposed hill ground. Even today more of the lower hill ground is being used for forestry and hill farming, and it is often fenced off from the deer, forcing them to live at higher altitudes on poor-quality land, and in what must be regarded as atypical places for them.

Communication and Locomotion

Red deer have highly developed senses of smell, sight and hearing. Their best known sound is the roar, or bell, which the stag makes during the rut. The roar is sometimes preceded or followed by several grunts. When animals are close together, such as at places where they are given extra winter food, they give low-pitched, soft grunts when approaching each other. The commonest calls of the hind are a gruff bark, and a low mooing bleat when trying to locate her young calf. The calf gives a nasal bleat to attract its mother or, if alarmed, a high-pitched squeal.

Hinds produce scent when they are in season, and the stag detects this by either smell or taste. There are other scent glands (the metatarsals on the hind leg, the tail, and the lachrymals below the eye) and these may be used in communication by marking areas during the rut, but we still know very little about how scent is used in the life of red deer.

Most communication between red deer is by sight, and they have developed a wide range of different behaviour patterns which are readily understood by other deer. When stags are being aggressive to one another they may raise the head with the ears lying flat, exposing the pale chin-patch, or perhaps tilt the head and antlers to one side. Hinds also use the former behaviour, but if the warning signal is not heeded a fight may ensue, and they go onto their hind legs and kick at a considerable rate with the forelegs. Stags fight like this when their antlers are in velvet and are likely to be damaged. When the antlers are hard, stags fight or spar by locking the antlers together and then twisting and pushing, using their strong neck and shoulder muscles to good advantage. They do not butt as goats and sheep do.

Red deer walk and trot, but when disturbed they canter and, for short distances, gallop. When suddenly alarmed, they move off with a series of stiff-legged jumps, bouncing on all four feet together. This adver-

Except when being fed, the calf is left lying alone for the first few days after birth. Its stillness and the camouflage given by its spotted coat are its protection from predators.

tises danger to other deer and the rump patch is also flared acting as a warning signal.

Red deer are capable swimmers and swim between

neighbouring islands. They are often seen swimming in the Bristol Channel, and those occasionally reported in Glamorgan are thought to have swum across from Somerset.

Social Structure

The sexes remain apart, living in different areas except during the mating season. Both stags and hinds live in groups, but the size of each group and its make-up varies from place to place.

Red deer society is based on a dominant female, or matriarch. She lives in a well defined area, which we call her home range, with her calf and possibly her calf of the previous year (her yearling). The calves start to explore before they are 6 months old and are independent by the time they are three years. How long they remain with the mother depends on whether she has more calves.

When a hind is about to give birth, she chases away her previous year's calf and only allows it back when her new calf is a couple of weeks old. Young stags at this time may form small bands or mix with groups of older stags. Those that return will be forced away again at the next rut by the master stag. Hinds have home ranges which overlap with their mother's, but the stags move away and live in different areas. So hinds in a group are likely to be related; stags in a group are not. Most deer, however, live fairly close to the areas where they were born and do not wander widely.

Red deer have adapted their basic social system to fit the range of different habitats where they live. In woodlands, groups are usually the family unit of hind, calf and yearling, and home ranges are small. On open ground it is different. In some areas, such as the island of Rhum in the western Highlands where red deer have been studied in great detail, the average size of groups in winter is 9, and the home ranges are still fairly small, being about 400 hectares for hinds and 800 hectares for stags. In the east and central Highlands the country is much more open and uniform, and groups average 30-40 with some individuals having home ranges up to 15 times the size of those on Rhum. It is on this open country that we see the really big herds of deer, and it is not uncommon to see groups of 500 or more. Groups of stags may be all young, or all old, or of mixed ages. Groups of hinds tend to have mainly milk hinds and calves, or yeld hinds and immature animals.

Yearly Cycle

After the rut the stags and hinds separate. In hill country the stags move down to lower parts of the moors or into woods and they use these all through the winter, but the hinds remain on the higher ground until bad weather and shortage of food force them onto the lower areas.

The areas used by stags and hinds are traditional, and a particular hillside or corrie will hold either one or the other, seldom will it hold both. Usually stags are found in the lowest part of the valleys and yeld hinds in the highest. Hinds eat more grasses than stags, and generally get better food in winter, their ranges lying over richer rocks. Stag areas usually have much more heather, but may also have better shelter.

It is interesting that the stags, who are certainly dominant to the hinds, do not use the best feeding areas. Hinds are pregnant and still suckling in late winter, so then at least they need good food. It would be nice to think that stags allow the hinds to use the better areas to ensure the survival of the calves, but it is difficult to see how such unselfish behaviour could

Hinds usually have only one calf; twins are very rare. While she is suckling, a hind eats twice her normal amount of food.

Although culling has increased over the last 20 years and fewer deer now die naturally, bad winters still take their toll.

Skeleton of stag.

evolve to the detriment of the individual stags. Perhaps stags need something else which is not found in the areas the hinds occupy, but nothing is really obvious.

In spring, when there is fresh growth of vegetation and better weather, stags and hinds move away from their wintering areas. The stags may stay on lower ground until July, but will move to higher places by August. Stags especially are pestered by insects in summer and may go to the very high, windier ground to get away from them. They will use these places until the rutting season, when they move back into the areas with hinds.

When not disturbed red deer feed throughout the day and night, but are particularly active around dawn and dusk. In woods where they are disturbed they become more nocturnal, staying in cover during the day and only venturing into the open at night to feed. In hill country they stay on the hillsides during the day but move down to feed on the lower grasslands at dusk, going up again around dawn.

Food and Feeding

Red deer live in many different habitats, so a wide variety of plants is eaten. The shoots and leaves of deciduous trees are their favourite foods, and grasses and herbs are very important, particularly in summer. In autumn and winter deer eat more heather (ling) on hill ground and in deciduous woods bramble, ivy and holly are much sought after. Ferns and lichens are also eaten and, near the coast, seaweeds, particularly kelps (*Laminaria* spp.).

Their feeding habits bring them into conflict with farmers and foresters. They eat some tree species in preference to others; oaks, aspens, rowans and willows are especially liked, whilst alders, birches and hornbeams are not. Amongst the conifers, Norway spruce, larch and Scots pine are preferred over lodgepole pine and Sitka spruce. Apart from browsing shoots, red deer also eat the bark of some trees, especially willows, rowans, Norway spruce and lodgepole pine. This can kill the tree if the wound is large or completely circles the trunk, or it opens the way for parasites and disease. Bark-stripping is a very serious problem and reduces the value of the timber being grown.

Disturbance

Red deer respond to disturbance in different ways according to the type of disturbance it is and where it occurs. On open-hill ground when a man is about, a hind with a calf of up to a few days old will leave it lying in cover and run off, often giving a gruff bark and using a high-stepping gait as if to draw him away. But if an eagle is hunting overhead, she quickly returns to the calf, and they both run off together. If necessary she turns and defends the calf against an eagle attack by going onto her hind legs and kicking with the forefeet. Red deer sometimes attack adders with the forefeet and I have seen fallow deer and sheep act similarly. There is an ancient tale from Pliny that stags draw serpents from their holes by their breath and then trample them to death!

When disturbed in hill country, they gallop off for a short distance, then walk quickly, usually in single file, away from the source of disturbance. The eventual leader is usually a mature milk hind in hind groups. In woodlands, though, they may lie down in thick cover or skirt around the source of disturbance rather than run ahead of it. It is generally very difficult to move deer out of their normal home area.

Although red deer are usually wary, they do become

Golden eagles kill only a small proportion of young calves each summer. Hinds are very protective to their calves when eagles are hunting and defend them vigorously.

accustomed to man, particularly if his activities are regular and not harmful to them. They quickly get used to coming to places where extra food is put out in winter, and really tame ones will soon eat from the hand.

Population Structure

Today, there is about 1 stag to every 1.3 hinds in Scotland. The sex ratio of embryos is about equal. Since the mid-1960's the main cause of death in Scottish red deer has been through shooting, and a kill of about one sixth of the adults is used as a guide to keep stocks steady. Before this date, few were shot, and many died of starvation. Death from starvation occurs mainly in calves and in the very old whose teeth are worn making feeding difficult. Nowadays, natural mortality generally accounts for less than 5% of all deaths.

One hears many old tales of stags living to several hundred years. There is an old Celtic poem which says:

Thrice the age of a dog is that of a horse
Thrice the age of a horse is that of a man
Thrice the age of a man is that of a deer
Thrice the age of a deer is that of an eagle

In fact, very few red deer live more than 20 years, and only about 10% of the population is over 8 years old.

Predators, Parasites and Disease

Since the wolf became extinct in the eighteenth century, adult red deer have had no natural enemies apart from man. A few newly-born calves are killed by golden eagles, but I know of no first-hand reports of foxes killing calves although they must be able to do so.

Wild deer are healthy and have few infectious diseases that kill them. Avian TB has been found but its effects are not known. Louping ill and tick-borne fever (rickettsial disease) are both carried but do not evidently affect them.

The main external parasites are ticks, deer keds, warble maggots, nostril maggots and lice. The head fly also irritate deer, particularly stags when their antlers are in velvet.

Of the internal parasites the liver fluke is widespread, and lungworms and tapeworms are also found.

Breeding

Red deer breed seasonally, and usually have single calves. In Britain there is only one proven case of twin births and very few cases of twin embryos. Sometimes a hind may be seen with more than one calf, but fostering could account for this, for milk hinds are very tolerant of other young calves.

Pregnancy lasts for about 235 days, and may be longer in bad winters when calves are also born lighter. A newly born male calf weighs about 6.7 kg and a female calf 6.4 kg on hill ground, but calves in woodlands are heavier. The main calving season is from mid-May to mid-June. Calves may suckle until just before the next calving season, particularly if the mother does not become pregnant again, but generally they are weaned at 4-8 months. When she is suckling, a hind increases the amount of food she eats by $2\frac{1}{2}$ times.

During the first days of life the calf lies alone, the mother returning only to feed it. At times, she can be several kilometres away from her calf, so finding a calf alone does not mean that it is orphaned. This is a common mistake made by trippers who misguidedly pick up such young deer. Usually within a week the calf

In September the stags become restless. The adult animals leave the all-male groups and go off on their own for a while before going to their favourite rutting areas.

Stags are fierce fighters during the rut when the hinds are at stake. Although injuries are frequent, deaths are not that common.

Mating in red deer is seldom seen. Hinds can breed as yearlings if conditions are favourable, but not usually before they are two or three years old on hill ground.

follows its mother and within two weeks or so they join the larger group.

In early September the mature stags leave the all male groups and move into areas occupied by hinds, where they round them up into harems. Adult stags tend to return to traditional, and quite localised, rutting areas.

The stag spends much energy keeping a harem together and fending off rival males. He does feed from time to time, but consumes only about half his normal intake; some stags are shot with completely empty stomachs. Whether a stag can hold a harem or not depends mainly on his age and his size. They are not usually capable of holding hinds during the main part of the rut (mid-September to the end of October) until they are 5 or 6 years old, but I have seen really big three-year-olds defend large harems. The average number of hinds and young in a harem varies from 10 to 15, but may be 70 or more.

The stag advertises himself to hinds or rival males by roaring, wallowing and rolling in his own ejaculum and urine (which helps give him the characteristic rank smell), and thrashing vegetation with his antlers. He stands in very exposed places where he would never be seen at other times. Fighting between stags during the rut is dramatic, but does not occur as often as one might believe. Most interactions between stags are ritualised and serious fighting is relatively uncommon, and only occurs between animals of equal size. Before fighting, the stags walk side by side, one then turns and lowers his head towards the rival and the pair lock antlers. Serious injuries from fighting do occur but deaths are infrequent, though occasionally two stags are found dead with their antlers locked together.

The chances of a hind being fertile depend very much on her condition, and, on open ground, only about 40% of the hinds breeding one year will become fertile the next. A hind does not usually reach breeding age until she is 2 or 3 years old on hill land in Scotland and south-west England, but yearlings can become pregnant if conditions are favourable. There is only one example of a female calf giving birth (i.e. at 12 months old) at a deer-park at Glenbuchat, Aberdeenshire. Unmated hinds have an oestrus cycle of about 18 days.

The number of calves born varies from around 56 per 100 hinds in deer-parks to 40-47 on open-hill land in Scotland. Some calves die at, or soon after, birth, probably because the mother had poor nutrition during the winter and spring when she was pregnant. She may be in such poor condition that she cannot give enough milk, or the calf may be born too weak to survive.

Importance to Man

Deer have always been important to man in some way. The remains of red deer are the commonest of all animals found at Mesolithic and Neolithic sites. He used the antlers and bones for tools, skins for clothing and, of course, the flesh for meat.

In early historical times many forests were reserved hunting areas, and the sport was jealously guarded. William the Conqueror of England was a passionate hunter, and anyone who killed a deer in the royal forests was executed. Even shooting at the deer and missing would result in the poacher's hands being cut off, or if deer were merely disturbed, the culprit was unceremoniously blinded. There are more than 100 deer-parks in Britain today, where deer are now kept mainly for amenity or for breeding purposes.

With the increase in livestock farming and forest clearances, deer numbers and range were greatly reduced in the Scottish lowlands in the fifteenth and sixteenth centuries and in the Highlands during the

In winter when food is scarce and the weather bad, squabbles frequently break out over a favoured feeding place.

Stags and hinds remain apart for most of the year, frequently living in different areas. Groups are biggest on open hill ground and smallest in woods.

Deer stalking is a traditional and important sport in the Highlands. The Highland pony is still the best way to extract the carcases from many parts of this wild and difficult country.

eighteenth and early nineteenth centuries. In the middle of the nineteenth century, however, sheep farming became less profitable, and deer-stalking became fashionable. That was the heyday of the deer-forest and lasted until the beginning of this century. Sheep and cattle farming became more important after the 1914-18 war, and people had less money to spend on maintaining large sporting estates. The conflict between deer and farming and forestry interests grew. Today more than £1 million per year is spent by the Forestry Commission in Scotland for forest protection and deer control alone, without considering the cost of damage done by the deer.

In order to safeguard the interests of farmers, foresters and the managers of deer, two Acts of Parliament have been passed, with various subsequent amendments: the Deer (Scotland) Act, 1959 and the Deer Act (1963) which applies to England and Wales. These designate close-seasons to shooting and hunting. In Scotland these are from 21st October to 30th June for stags and 16th February to 20th October for hinds, and in England and Wales from 1st May to 31st July for stags and 1st March to 31st October for hinds. Shooting in England and Wales is also limited by firearms specifications.

But, despite being a pest, red deer are also a resource, as an amenity and as a source of meat and sport. There is an increasing interest in deer stalking in Scotland, particularly from sportsmen from the European continent. The market in venison is also increasing and 42,000 carcases are now exported annually. In fact, there is now so much interest in red deer as another source of meat that attempts are being made to farm them on a commercial scale. An experimental farm was set up in Scotland in 1970 to see if intensive deer farming was practical. This gave encouraging results, so that many commercial farms have now started up. Perhaps red deer have finally come full-circle from being a mainstay of Neolithic man to a new domesticated animal. But whatever the outcome of intensive farming, the wild red deer will undoubtedly remain as one of the grandest members of our native fauna, and one which reminds us that, despite man's destruction of habitats, some mammals can, and do, readily adapt and survive. It will surely live up to Landseer's famous painting in being the 'Monarch of the Glen'.

A deer farm in Scotland. Once a major food of Neolithic man, red deer are now being farmed in several parts of the world.